ANIMALS GROWING UP

HOW ELEPHANTS GROW UP

Enslow Publishing
101 W. 23rd Street
Suite 240
New York, NY 10011
USA
enslow.com

Heather Moore Niver

WORDS TO KNOW

calf The young of elephants or other large mammals.

herbivore An animal that eats plants.

herd A large group of animals that lives together.

mammal An animal that has a backbone and hair; the females usually give birth to live babies and produce milk to feed their young.

matriarch The female leader of a group.

nurse To feed a baby milk produced from the body.

predator An animal that kills and eats other animals to stay alive.

pregnant Having a baby inside the body.

wean To change a baby from drinking its mother's milk to eating other food.

CONTENTS

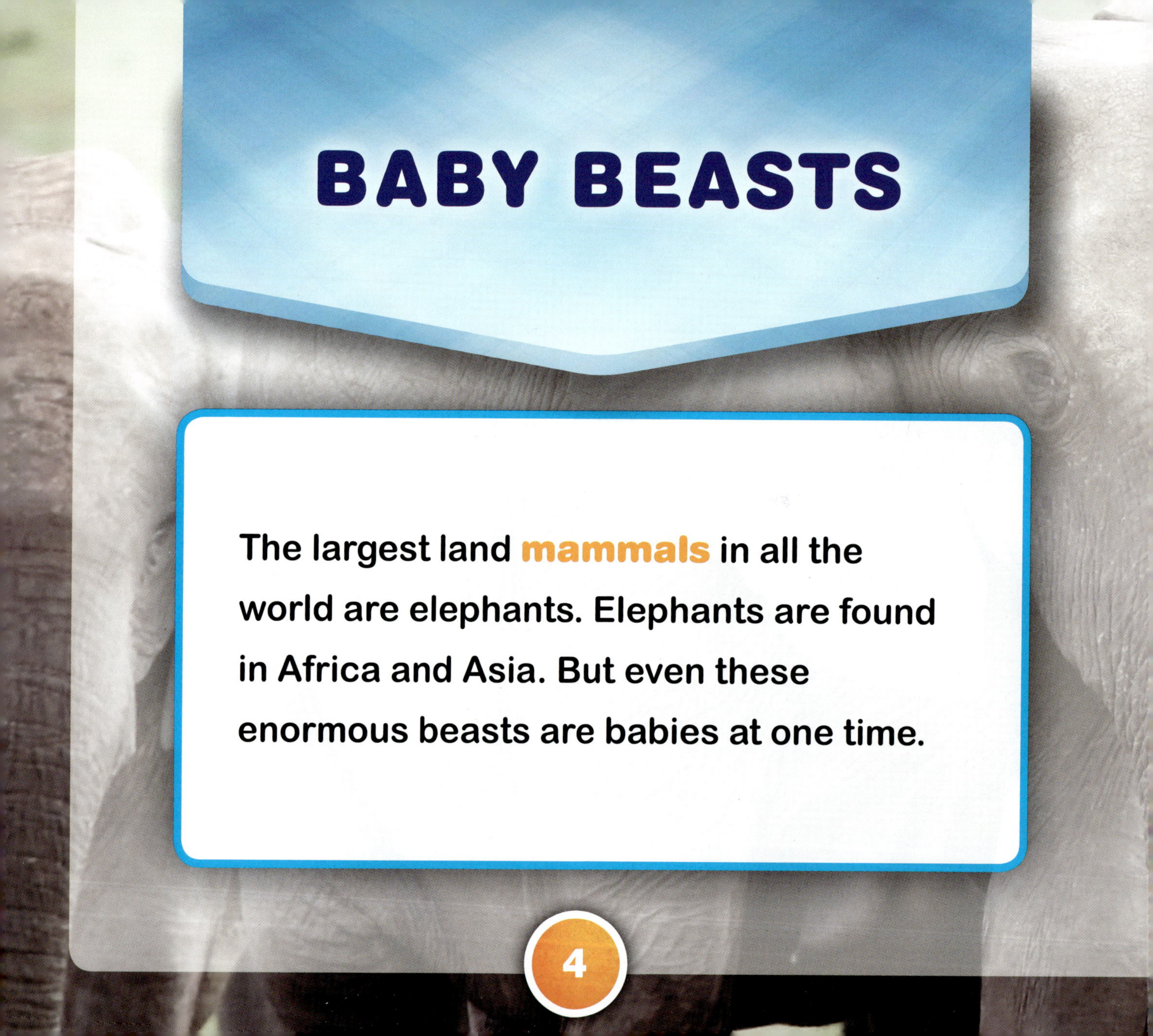

BABY BEASTS

The largest land **mammals** in all the world are elephants. Elephants are found in Africa and Asia. But even these enormous beasts are babies at one time.

FAST FACT

African elephants are a little larger than Asian elephants.

Asian elephants (*left*) have smaller ears than African elephants (*right*).

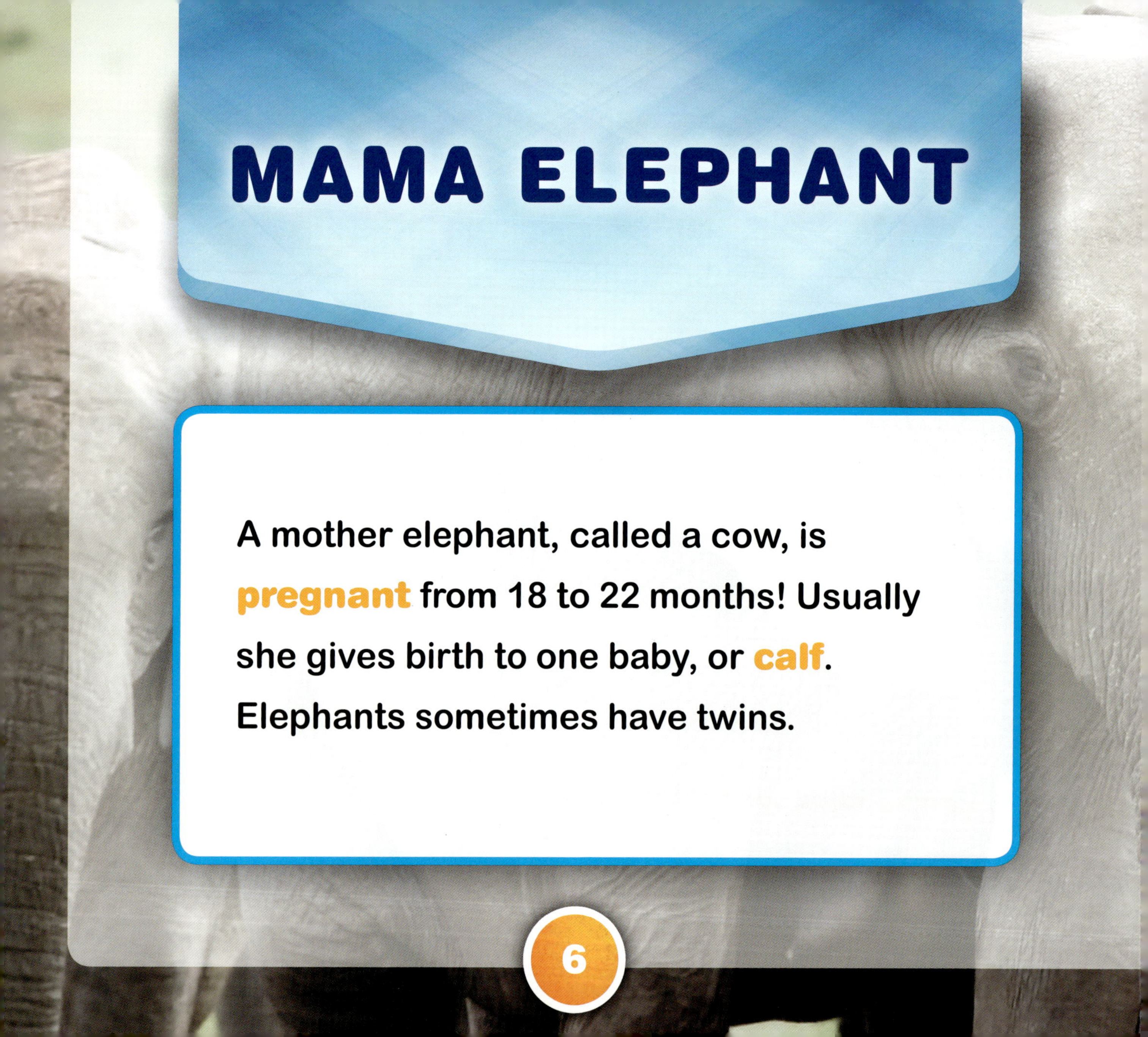

MAMA ELEPHANT

A mother elephant, called a cow, is **pregnant** from 18 to 22 months! Usually she gives birth to one baby, or **calf**. Elephants sometimes have twins.

FAST FACT

Females usually have calves once every four or five years.

A pregnant Asian elephant walks with her older calf.

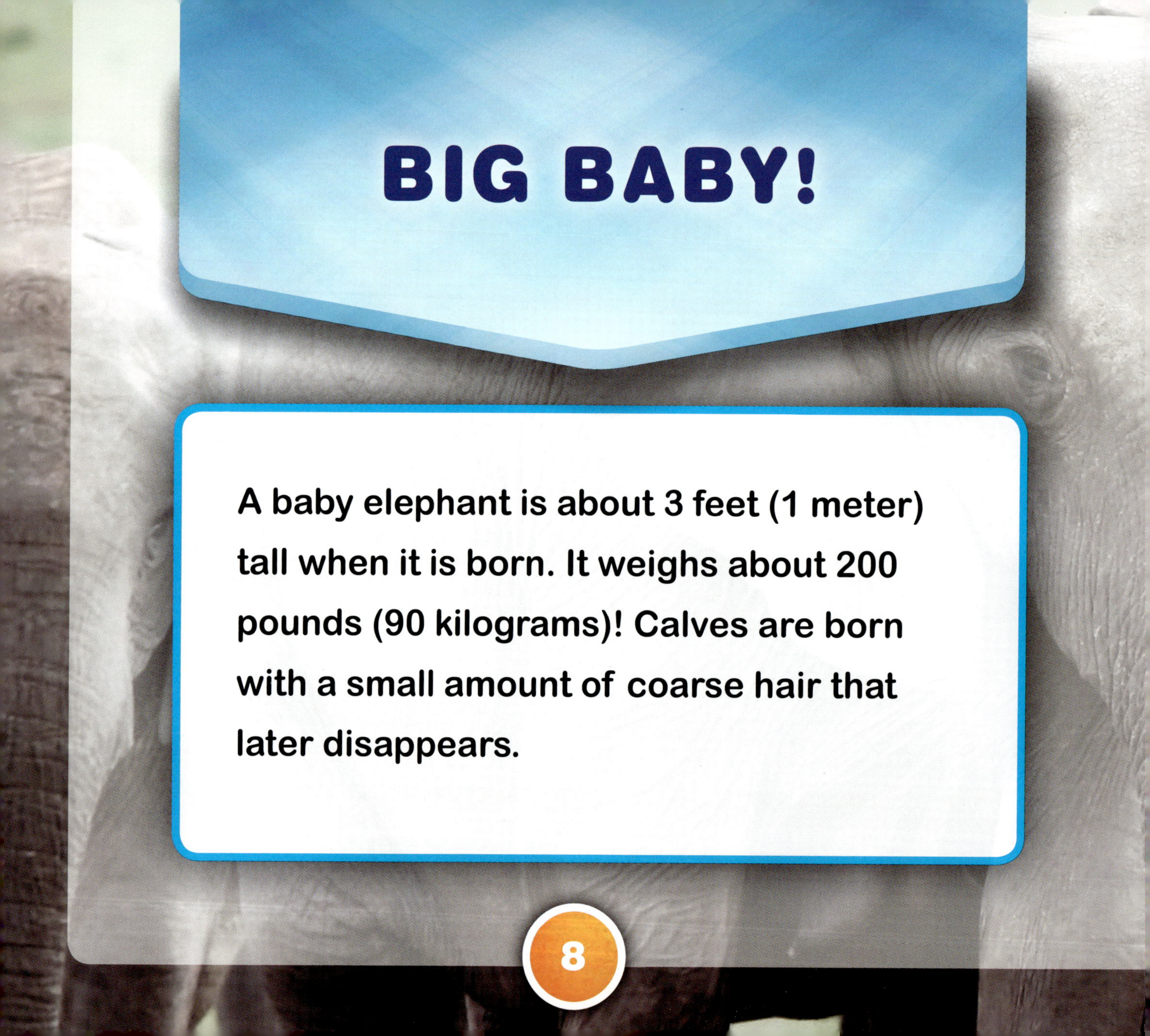

BIG BABY!

A baby elephant is about 3 feet (1 meter) tall when it is born. It weighs about 200 pounds (90 kilograms)! Calves are born with a small amount of coarse hair that later disappears.

FAST FACT

Elephants usually live about 60 years in the wild. They can live 80 years in zoos.

A newborn Asian elephant calf has black hair all over its body.

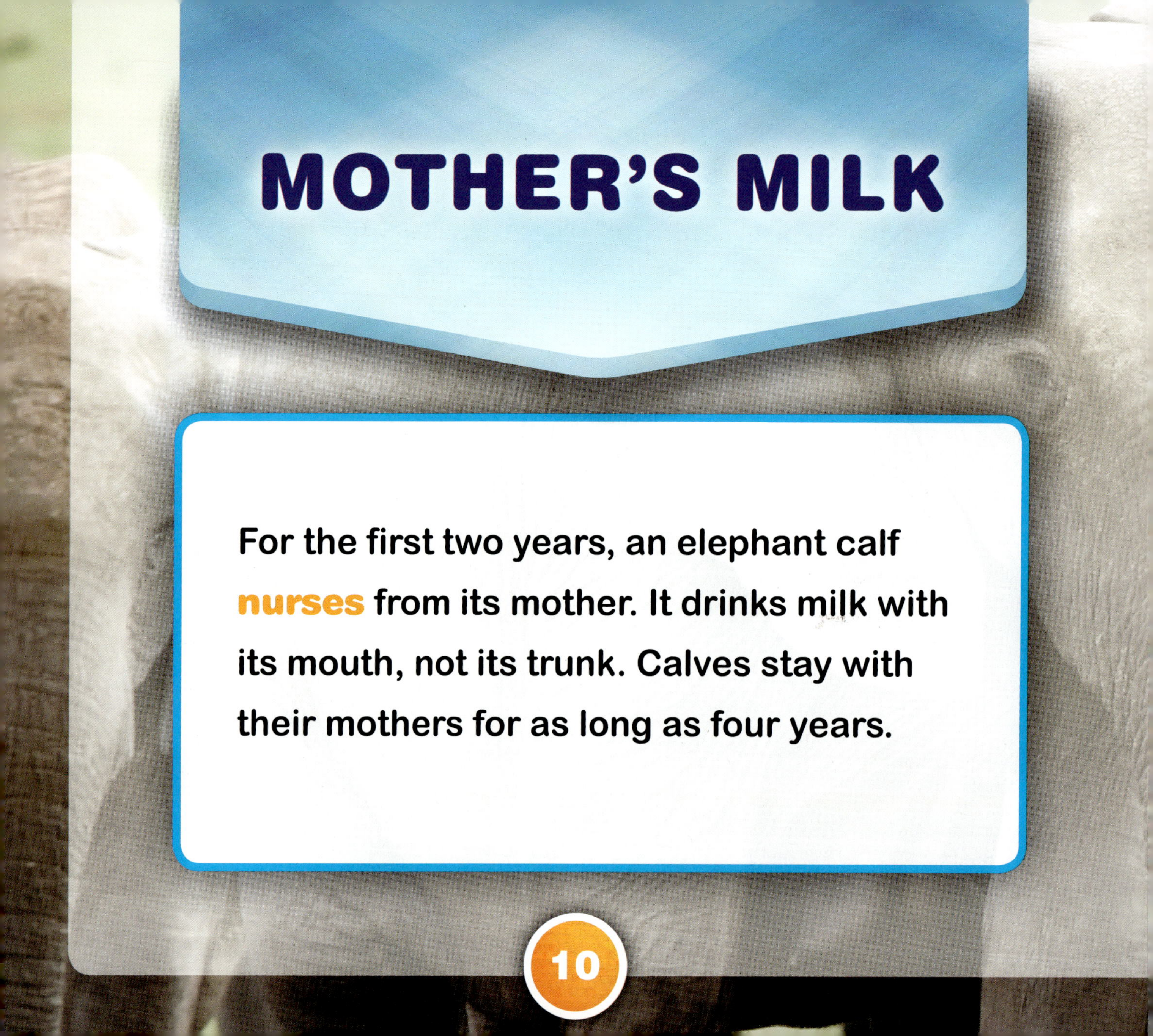

MOTHER'S MILK

For the first two years, an elephant calf **nurses** from its mother. It drinks milk with its mouth, not its trunk. Calves stay with their mothers for as long as four years.

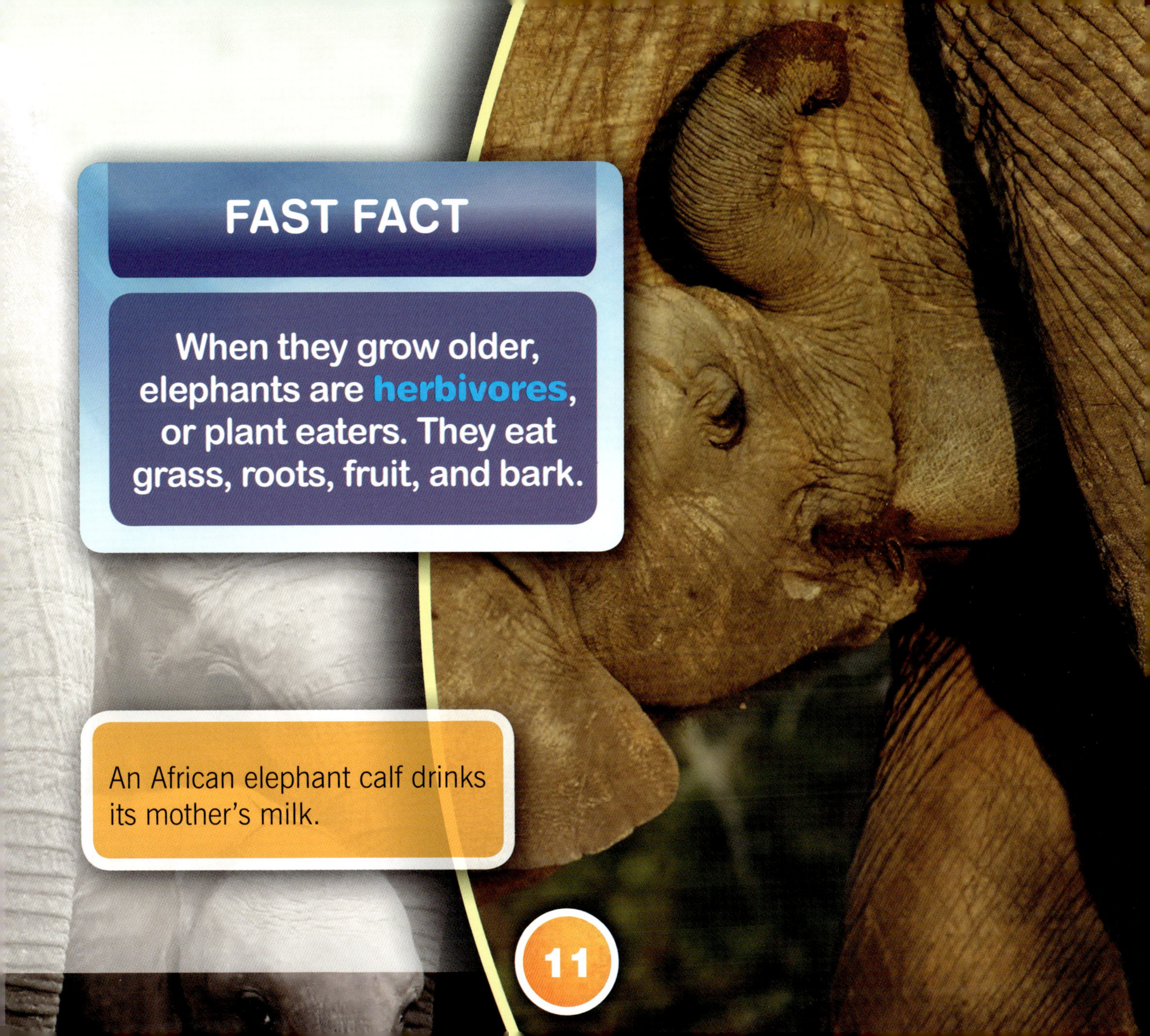

FAST FACT

When they grow older, elephants are **herbivores**, or plant eaters. They eat grass, roots, fruit, and bark.

An African elephant calf drinks its mother's milk.

BABY DAYS

Elephant calves have a lot to learn. They spend their days learning to make all four legs work together to walk. They even practice spreading their ears out wide.

An African elephant helps her newborn calf stand up and learn to walk.

FAST FACT

Baby elephants are clumsy and have to learn how to use their trunks, too.

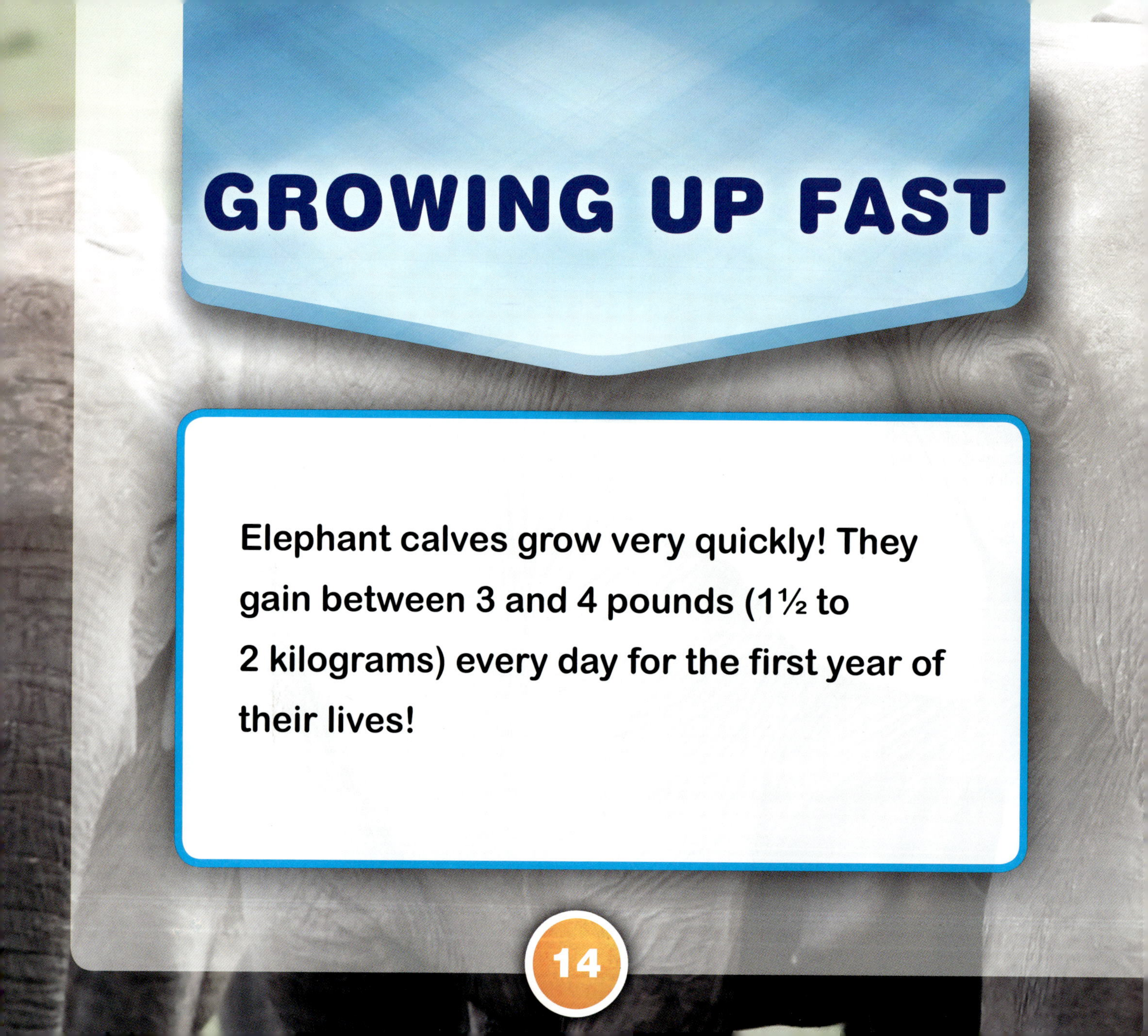

GROWING UP FAST

Elephant calves grow very quickly! They gain between 3 and 4 pounds (1½ to 2 kilograms) every day for the first year of their lives!

FAST FACT

Adult elephants may eat as much as 300 pounds (136 kilograms) of food in just one day!

An African elephant calf grows healthy and strong. It runs to a water hole.

FAMILY

When elephants are no longer nursing, they are **weaned**. Males, called bulls, go off on their own. Female elephants stay with their mothers and the **herd**.

FAST FACT

Baby elephants stay close to adults to stay safe from **predators** such as hyenas, lions, leopards, or crocodiles.

A herd of African elephants protects the young calves as they walk.

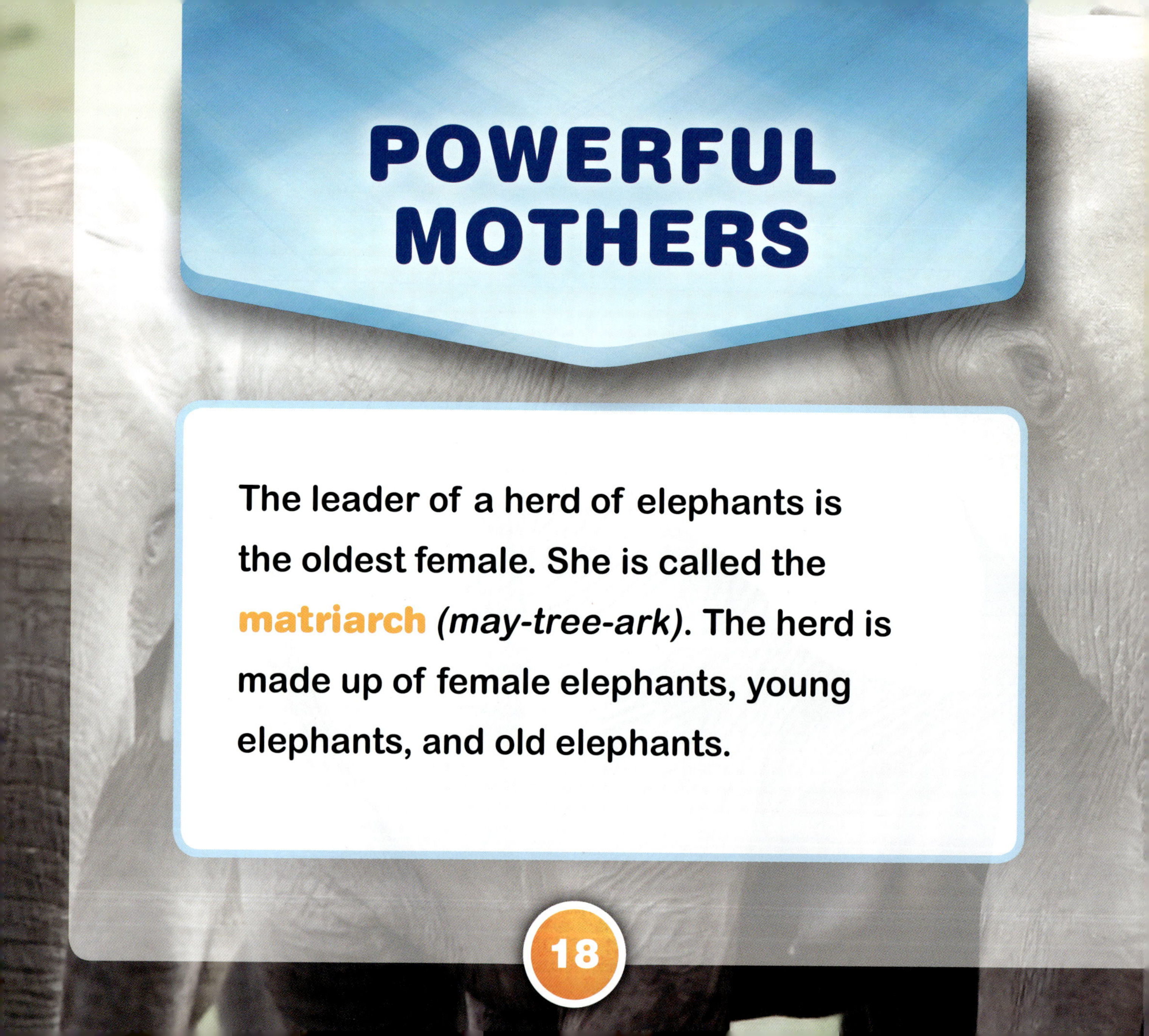

POWERFUL MOTHERS

The leader of a herd of elephants is the oldest female. She is called the **matriarch** *(may-tree-ark)*. The herd is made up of female elephants, young elephants, and old elephants.

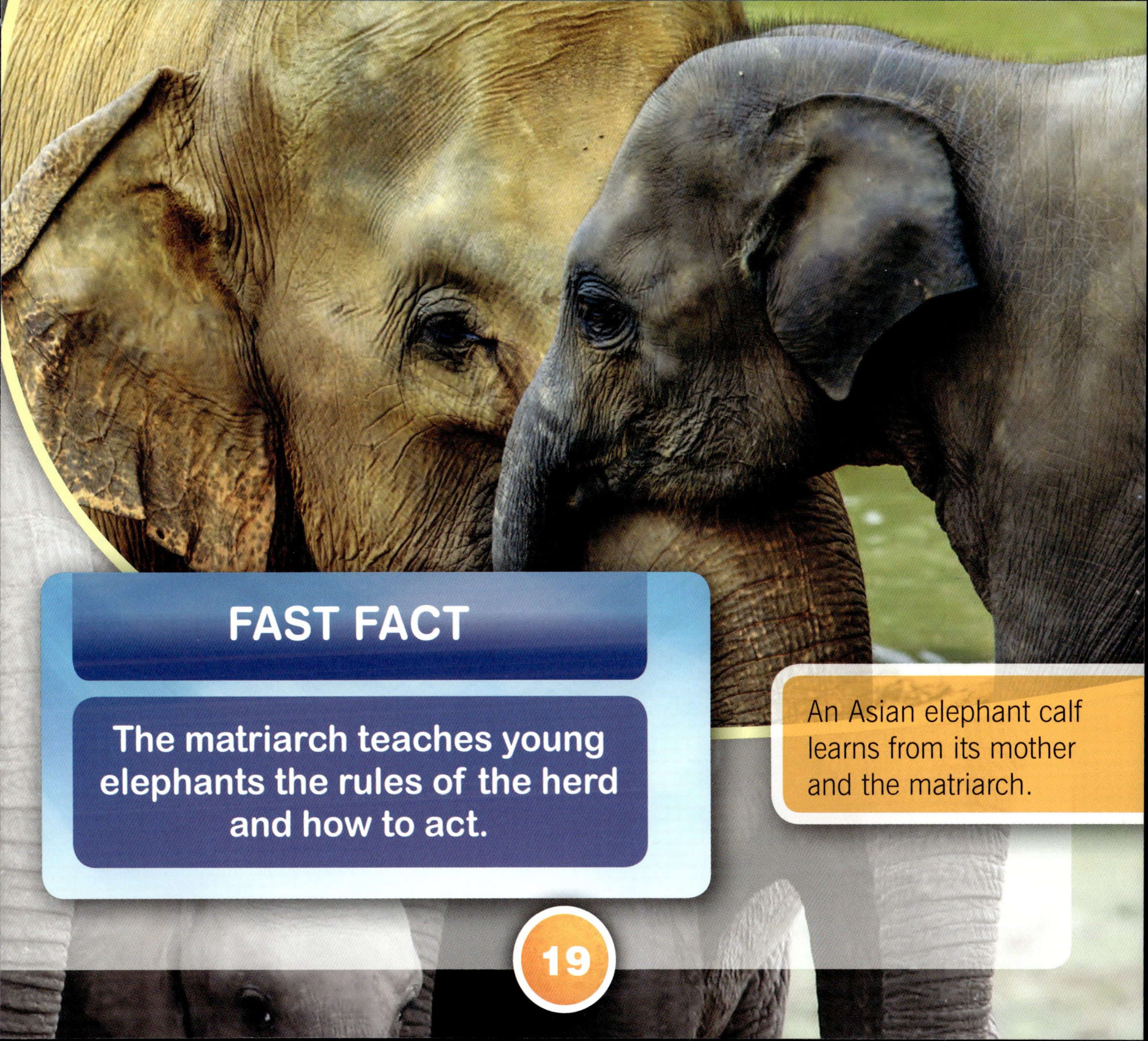

FAST FACT

The matriarch teaches young elephants the rules of the herd and how to act.

An Asian elephant calf learns from its mother and the matriarch.

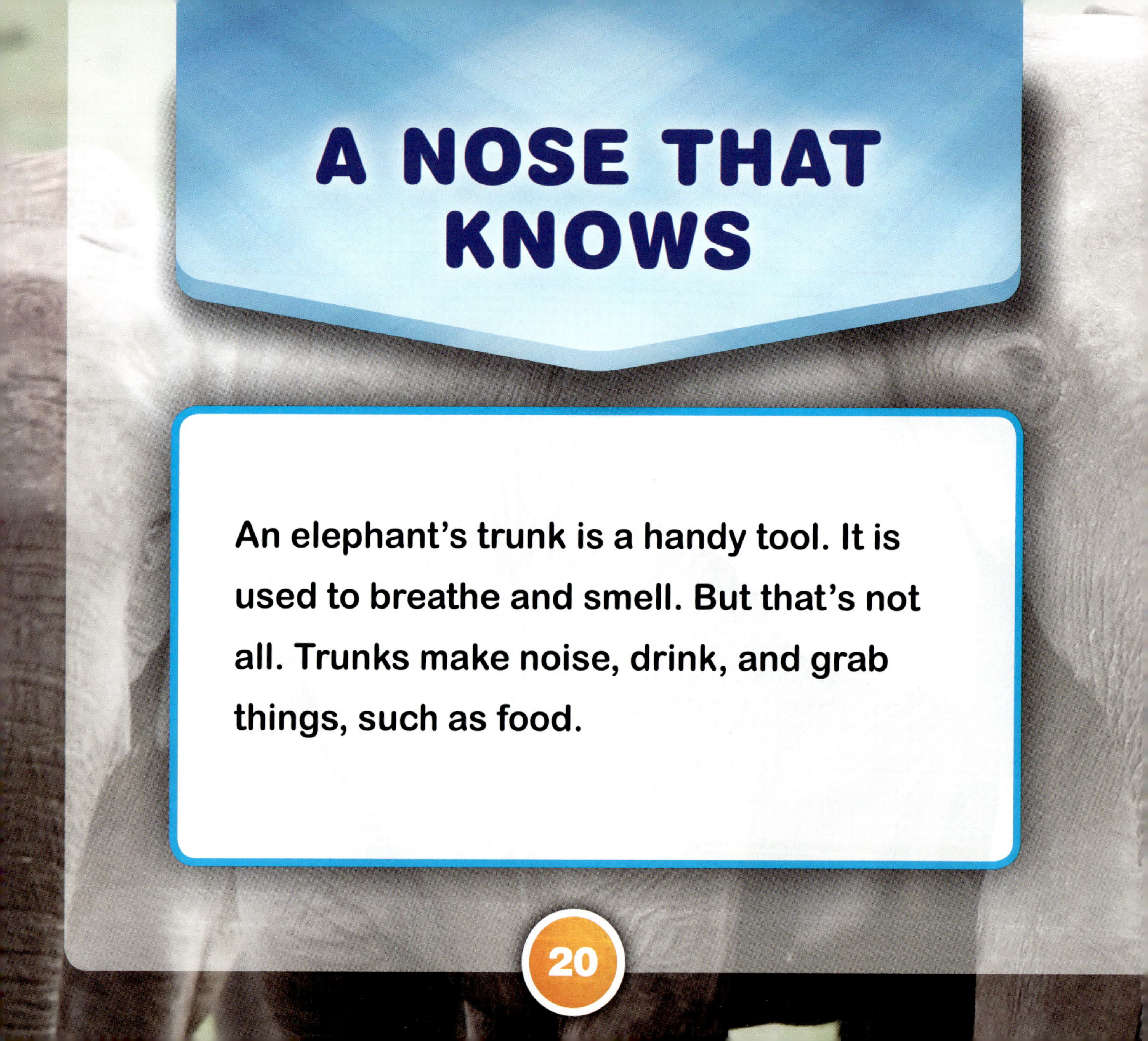

A NOSE THAT KNOWS

An elephant's trunk is a handy tool. It is used to breathe and smell. But that's not all. Trunks make noise, drink, and grab things, such as food.

FAST FACT

The elephant's trunk is made up of 100,000 different muscles!

An African elephant calf uses its trunk to pick leaves from a tree.

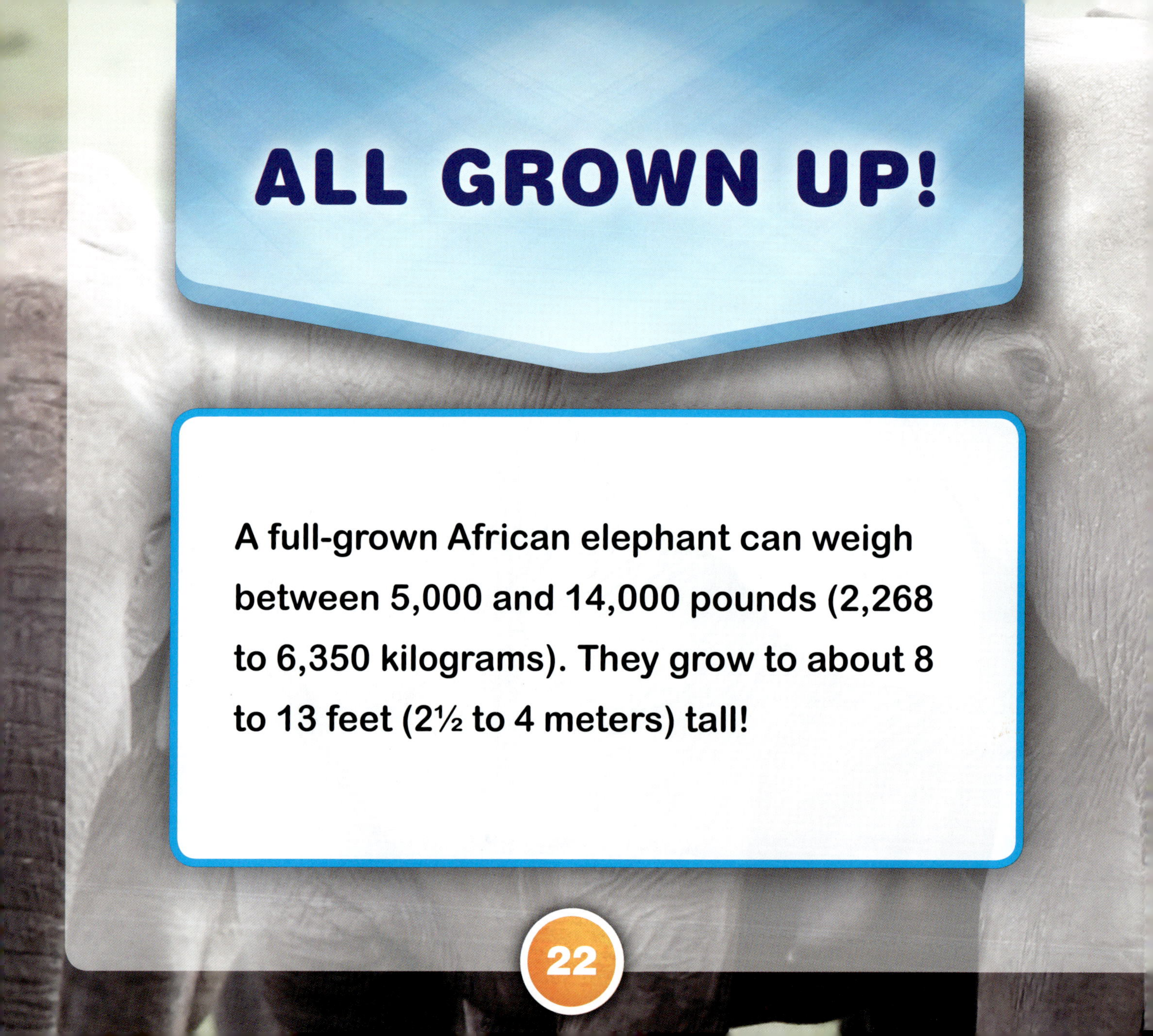

ALL GROWN UP!

A full-grown African elephant can weigh between 5,000 and 14,000 pounds (2,268 to 6,350 kilograms). They grow to about 8 to 13 feet (2½ to 4 meters) tall!

An Asian elephant herd takes a dip in the water.

FAST FACT

When they are between 13 and 20 years old, female elephants can have their own babies.

LEARN MORE

Books

Kelley, K. C. *Baby Elephants*. Mankato, MN: Amicus, 2018.

Leaf, Christina. *Baby Elephants*. Minneapolis, MN: Bellwether Media, 2015.

O'Connell, Caitlin, and T. C. Rodwell. *A Baby Elephant in the Wild*. New York, NY: Houghton Mifflin Harcourt, 2014.

Websites

San Diego Zoo Kids: African Elephant
kids.sandiegozoo.org/animals/african-elephant
Learn about African elephants and how they are different from Asian elephants!

National Geographic Kids: Asian Elephant
kids.nationalgeographic.com/animals/asian-elephant/#three-asian-elephants.jpg
Read fascinating facts about Asian elephants.

INDEX

Published in 2019 by Enslow Publishing, LLC.
101 W. 23rd Street, Suite 240, New York, NY 10011

Library of Congress Cataloging-in-Publication Data
Names: Niver, Heather Moore, author.
Title: How elephants grow up / Heather Moore Niver.
Description: New York, NY : Enslow Publishing, 2019. | Series: Animals growing up | Includes bibliographical references and index. | Audience: Grades K to 3.
Identifiers: LCCN 2017045118| ISBN 9780766096431 (library bound) | ISBN 9780766096448 (pbk.) | ISBN 9780766096455 (6 pack)
Subjects: LCSH: Elephants—Development—Juvenile literature. | Elephants—Infancy—Juvenile literature.
Classification: LCC QL737.P98 N578 2017 | DDC 599.6713/92—dc23
LC record available at https://lccn.loc.gov/2017045118

Printed in the United States of America

Photos Credits: Cover, p. 1 Enn Li Photography/Moment/Getty Images; pp. 4–23 (background image), 11, 15, 17 Four Oaks/Shutterstock.com; p. 5 (left) Alexandr Junek Imaging/Shutterstock.com; p. 5 (right) paula french/Shutterstock.com; p. 7 © MikaelEriksson/iStock/Thinkstock; p. 9 Natalia Kolesnikova/AFP/Getty Images; p. 13 Auscape/Universal Images Group/Getty Images; p. 19 Zhukova Valentyna/Shutterstock.com; p. 21 PilArt/Shutterstock.com; p. 23 Honza Hruby/Shutterstock.com.